HOUSE OF THE LEFT-HAND DOOR

URSULA KIERNAN

Slipstream Books

Published by:

Slipstream Books
Willowbank
16a Lower Street
Pulborough
W. Sussex RH20 2BL

WEST SUSSEX LIBRARY SERVICE

0094748

Copyright ©Ursula Kiernan 2005

All rights reserved. No part of this publication may be reproduced, stored in a retrieval system, or transmitted in any form or by any means, electronic, mechanical, photocopying, recording or otherwise, without the prior permission of the copyright holders.

A CIP catalogue record for this book is available from The British Library

ISBN 0-9544404-1-2

Slipstream Books

Designed and typeset by:

Cherrybite Publications
Linden Cottage
45 Burton Road
Little Neston
CH64 4AE
Tel: 0151 353 0967
www.cherrybite.co.uk
e-mail: helicon@globalnet.co.uk

Dedication:
to Slipstream Poets
and the tutors and colleagues
I have worked with
and learnt from.

Cover illustration by Emmanuel Antwi-Bawuah, 3rd Form, Christ's Hospital, loosely based on a drawing of the Chinese God of the Left-Hand Doorway, in *Larousse Encyclopedia of Mythology,* Paul Hamlyn Ltd 1959.

Acknowledgements are due to the editors of
Cadenza, Envoi, Krax and Tears in the Fence.
Three poems were first published in Fish That Sing:
National Poetry Foundation.

COMMUNICATING DOORS

COMMUNICATING DOORS

Considering Newts	7
The Football	8
Tunley Cottage	9
A House Divided	10
The House in Hove	11
Joy-Riding	12
Going For Gold	14
Glebe Fields	15
Hurrah For Harvest Home	16
Crash	17
Wild Justice	18
Whipp's Circus	20
Walking through Woods	21
Home Sweet Home	22
House Beautiful	23
Communicating Doors	24
The Good Life	26

CONSIDERING NEWTS

The newts I liked best had spiky crests. All
had velvety skin, wavy tails, neat little snouts
and intelligent eyes; and such elegant elbows,
such delicate claws. In Spring some males
had orange bellies with silver-blue tail stripes.

I would squat on the bank or more often wade in,
dress bunched in knickers, defying mosquitos,
hot lumpy nights. The water was cool and clear
further out. But always that thick black slime
at the edges was waiting to clutch my bare legs.

Newts were an important part of my childhood.
I spent hours watching them, catching them,
taking them home in glass jars, drawing them,
making scrupulous notes. I remember with shame
how often I let those frail creatures escape,

they'd turn up days later, just bags of skin.
I could only stare at the runaways, wanting
to put back the flesh. But what did newts eat?
Today hardly any children go fishing in streams.
Why bother when Google will fill their net?

THE FOOTBALL

Was I cast for bitchdom as young as seven?
Or were you a natural butt for my wit,
doting on Alistair Cooke as you did, praying
a lot, and climbing upstairs on all fours?

Hard to believe you were once tough and burly.
Rumour has it you toppled a Guardsman
the day you collided on Battersea Bridge;
but I only knew you as old and wheezy.

I hated your sourey under-arm smell; your rusty
mauve clothes; your high-buttoned gaiters;
that ludicrous hat with the veil and cherries.
I detested having to cut your toenails.

But your Christmas presents were inspirational.
A mouse and a wheel. A gold lacquer stool.
A Chinese kite. Then the football I craved;
but Dad said no, and back it went to the shop.

Hans Andersen brought us our closest moments.
I climbed on your knee to be read to then,
sometimes pretending a cough or sore throat;
blackcurrant jujubes were sure to emerge.

Look Gran, it's a bit late I know but I'm sorry
my discontent spilled over you, though you seemed
to accept it as fair. My brother had three or four
footballs. I had to have something to kick.

TUNLEY COTTAGE

"You won't need that gas-mask!" was Florrie's first remark.
Tunley Cottage smelt of beeswax and warm soda-bread;
water came up in a bucket when you wound a handle;
in the orchard dead rooks hung as warnings, all strange

to a London child. Stranger still, a path led through black
currant bushes to an outdoor privy. Sunday night
was bath night. Florrie poured hot water in a galvanised
tin tub. Ellen loved the glow of firelight from the copper.

How George cherished those brass paraffin lamps; they never
failed or smelt. Florrie bottled plums and pears, sealing
the jars with wax. Her washing was first out on Monday;
her sunflowers were the tallest. Once Ellen was sent home

from school with a 'dirty' head. Florrie hugged her first,
then expertly plied a fine steel comb. She and George
were listening to the wireless with anxious faces. Till now,
the war had seemed a long way off. Soon afterwards

a German plane came down in flames only three fields away.
They stopped her looking at the wreckage, but they couldn't
stop her ears. It was one of those plaguey Messerschmitts;
the pilot's neck was broken, and him still in his teens!

But surely he was German and a baddie? Yet they seemed
to care about him, these tall Cotswold women with sons
his age. That was the summer George killed over thirty
adders. And Ellen, being fitted for a new school dress,

blushed to see her nipples rise like halma pieces
under the blue gingham. "My, you're a proper little woman!"
Florrie teased. Next day they took the bus to Stroud
....and Ellen chose that first feather-light teen bra.

A HOUSE DIVIDED

I was Dad's best girl until I had to go and spoil it all —
until I guilelessly pulled up my top
to show him my first bra.

Suddenly my skirt was far too short, my hair too long.
My tights annoyed him on the line;
he'd swat at them in passing.

The first time Philip walked me home from school
Dad turned puce. Girls who led lads on
only got what they deserved.

He pruned our gooseberry bushes bare that summer
as if their greenery might conceal
some shameful intimation.

Mum told him to relax, <u>enjoy</u> my dandelion days;
not try to put a grown-up head
on teenage shoulders.

I pushed my luck. Late back from my first dance
...and lingering on the doorstep
snogging Philip Spence.

Dad was waiting for me. I almost fainted when he dropped
his trousers. But I still obeyed him:
I looked...I even touched.

Afterwards Dad wore Mum's bruises with defiant pride.
Hadn't it been a timely warning
of fires that may consume young girls!

Years passed before I dared life afresh with Philip.
The marriage fell apart; we always felt
Dad looking on.

And then, I didn't have home-making skills. I tried hard
to be like Mum, but Father
always stared back from my mirror.

I'm failing as a mother now. Can't cope with louts in leather,
all bent on making it with Fleur
who's just sixteen and knows she's stunning.

Today the *Interflora* van delivered twenty-four red roses.
Has she lowered her guard already?
Mum says our Fleur

is not that sort of girl. Dad says all girls are the same;
best keep her under lock and key
before she leads some decent lad astray.

THE HOUSE IN HOVE

I knew I'd been acting too tight, too controlled;
it was finding the small wax candles
that finally loosened my tears —
three Birthday candles and a brown curl
wrapped in white tissue paper
and treasured for years.

Then I discovered the folder of paintings
fastened with ribbon and labelled
Marmalade Cat, Bramber Castle, Picnic
at Climping, Dick Turpin, a Snake —
with my own age recorded
not only in years but in months.

How could the mother who'd loved us so much
have become just a lap for stray cats —
a person who didn't give prezzies on birthdays
and forgot all her grandchildren's names?
And then, when they read out her Will,
the name she'd forgotten was mine.

JOY-RIDING

"The end is where we start from." T.S. Eliot

I

So now I'm crossed off as a foster mother,
having failed to wean you away from the notion
that everything falls off a lorry.

I blame television; the focus on smooth
anti-heroes, dodgy dealing
the endless display, cars as icons.

You're only twelve, so how could you know
these were the wrong role models?
It's plain you can't help

having sticky fingers, but they plan to uproot you
just the same; send you to a secure unit.
No joy-riding there!

Oh but life will be thinner without you;
I've grown used to your crazy
excuses, your smudgy grin.

Quick child, before they come for you,
let's take one last joy-ride together
in this gold-bronze Jaguar,

trust this purring beast to chase the tail of time,
rush cat-like down dim Motor Ways,
till concrete fades and forests rise again.

II

Child, I see leaves and sky reflecting
in your eyes while you gather roots and berries.
One day you'll join the hunters;

in the meantime you're learning to make fire;
strip fur from animals; settle in caves;
paint the walls with antelopes and aurochs.

For now, you squat contentedly with other juveniles
listening to the honoured story-makers
spinning the magical tale of the tribe.

How long before you start to yawn, feel restless
develop itchy feet? Demand a frame
that stretches you, a livelier horizon?

III

What's the point of history, you ask?
Bright kids like you, survivors,
deserve sharp mobile phones, digital cameras.

Last member of a defunct clan, you've now
forgotten how to hunt, your stories
come courtesy of the media

that tells of strange foods, global warming,
ignores taboos and all the old ways.
What's this! The anti-heroes back again?

As for those tiresome little household gods
that used to hang from doorways,
it looks as if they've fled.

Now there's football and pop stars to worship:
instant fame. Watch it, child,
you could have your fifteen minutes too!

GOING FOR GOLD

You pile more cream on top of damson jam,
Try hard to squeeze in one more home-made scone,
Incline towards a cheese-bite topped with ham.
The Size Ten girl I loved so much has gone,
You pile more cream on top of damson jam.

How long since we two shared our lecture-notes?
Not then Earl Grey sipped from a china cup;
Then, Undergraduates wore Duffle coats,
Read Dom Moraes and Kaddish standing up.
How long since we two shared our lecture-notes?

Some things still hurt in the remembering.
You pitied me my childhood spent in care,
Not so, your family in Angmering:
I had no class, no cash, no *savoir-faire*.
Some things still hurt in the remembering.

Perhaps our marriage plans should wait a while.
'Be gentle darling, not so fast!' you'd plead;
I see it still, that tear-bright wobbly smile,
'Don't touch me there. Remember, <u>we agreed!</u>'
Perhaps our marriage plans should wait a while.

Were we too young to put our love on hold?
I told myself your parents were to blame
But it was I who chose to go for gold
And bedded those two harpies, wealth and fame.
We <u>were</u> too young to put our love on hold.

GLEBE FIELDS

Well may you hang your head, my beauty;
I've not forgotten the hole you tore
in my red crimplene pants;
taking the seat right out.

Surely you don't get your kicks from frightening
the simple folk of Storrington
who like to walk their dogs
through the Glebe Fields of St. Mary's?

No, I won't saddle you with meanness.
I recognise you as an activist and agitator;
there's logic in those tragic sighs,
the hunch of your heavy shoulders.

First you trample, then roll over
on their insensate plans
to build on land where horses
always grazed like kings;

snorting and running, heaving
steaming chestnut flanks
as they stand and raise
their bronze heads to the gods.

It has always been this way;
but now come the developers,
pile drivers, concrete mixers —
don't let them pour gravel in your soul.

HURRAH FOR HARVEST-HOME

The harvest's in! Time now for celebration!
The whirling blades have claimed their sacrifice:
Alas the waste, the soul-less mutilation.

My niece has had a city education;
Unused to farms, she's free with her advice.
The harvest's in! Time now for celebration!

We need to thin the rabbit population
But her small hand in mine fast turns to ice.
Alas the waste, the soul-less mutilation.

This leg should have immediate amputation!
'It's just a stoat. I'll kill it in a trice.'
The harvest's in! Time now for celebration!

Larks' eggs grown cold arouse more indignation.
Against the rich ripe corn, a trifling price;
Alas the waste, the soul-less mutilation.

She talks of 'habitat' and 'conservation',
Despairs about a nest of harvest mice.
The harvest's in! Time now for celebration!

My red-stained hands cause further perturbation;
All townsfolk are like this, too overnice!
Alas the waste, the soul-less mutilation.

Hard work goes into harvest decoration;
Corn garlands gleam; the plaiting is precise.
The harvest's in! Time now for celebration!
Alas the waste, the soul-less mutilation.

CRASH

I hope you never sneer at rhino!
These beasts are neither deaf nor blind.
Perhaps this lumbering thick-skinned fellow
is shy about his huge behind.

It's true that one can see and smell
the dung-pile of rhinoceros
for in excess of half a mile —
so gross it is and odoriferous.

We might decide he's somewhat large
for such close confines as Longleat.
Can we be sure he'll halt his charge
before he tramples on our feet?

We're told his nature's rather mild
considering all that's on his mind,
like his poor cousins in the wild
so cruelly poached by humankind.

Bad men de-horn the slaughtered creature
to make up aphrodisiacs.
How would you like *your* horny feature
to feel that unrelenting axe?

WILD JUSTICE

The train is going to Gloucester Road. The girl too
is going round in circles. She's picked weirdo
fellow-passengers; you could say *other worldly*
but for their briefcases and dark glasses.

The man with the designer suit and Dürer hands
asks if she's in trouble. Blushing furiously
she tells him no, nothing special, not today;
although it bothers her sometimes, this sense of sin.

She blames herself too much, he thinks; after all
she can't be more than, say, sixteen. She's reads
a lot, she tells him. First the Classics; Dickens,
Scott...and more recently, the meatier stuff.

Journey to Ixtlan half-way through. Salman
Rushdie waiting at the library. She risks a smile;
he's rather nice. If only she could see his eyes.
He hesitates when asked his name,

call him Rogozhin or Karamazov, something old
and dark and physical. Rasputin even. He speaks
of global warming; vanished habitats; Siberian
bears; the rare black rhino; seal pups clubbed

on sparkling snow. "I've been there!" she says.
In her mind's eye, she means. Teenagers aren't
good witnesses. At last, the crux. *She's seen
a fox's brush held high, a child blooded.*

"And somehow you're to blame! But aren't you
being a bit grandiose? Your back's too slim
for such a monstrous load." It clings to her though
like a Siamese twin. He takes off his specs,

his eyes are charred holes. "We've moved on
since Sunday church and hunt protesters.
Civil war broke out upstairs. They crucified
St. Peter and the old guard." This guy's seriously

off the wall. She inches cautiously a little further
down the seat but his crazy talk pursues her.
"That chap you knew as God has gone. Snipers
got him and his son, on their way to church.

"Old Gorilla is God now. He's lost his hands,
they're ash-trays somewhere in Japan. Revenge
addles his decisions; he's got it in for humans.
There's no appeal of course. He's above the law."

Only one thing matters now and that's to get
to Gloucester Road.....rejoin the real world.
But this, she has to know. "You and all your
funny friends, what happened to your eyes?"

"We paid the reckoning Child, as you will do
when your turn comes. They blind you first
to teach you how to see, then they eat you
from the inside out, leaving only the skin.

"A briefcase though will keep you grounded."
She's so disoriented now that people stare
when she gets off at Gloucester Road.
Then someone says "What's eating this poor girl?"

WHIPP'S CIRCUS

We've been to Stratford, done the sights;
toured London
in a double-decker.

Fed up with travelling, we'll sit back tonight,
hope for laughter at the circus,
perhaps thrills.

We yawn at poodles dressed in drawers
and sequinned ladies
on high wires;

but as that troupe of pale fawn ghosts glides in
our nostrils flare, our eyes
are raging furnaces.

Whip and chair are flung aside, the trainer jumps
through his own hoops. The lions
stare bemused.

Things have gone badly wrong. This isn't what
the public paid to see. A lady
leaves her seat.

She'll sort those big cats out! The iron cage
disintegrates; it isn't used
to being rattled.

Ah Mr. Whipp, you've lost your lions,
they're going home to Ethiopia. And not
just running, *flying*.

Shouting's a waste of breath:
lions only start to hear
once you've invited them into your heart.

WALKING THROUGH WOODS

I struggle this time to climb the hill.
Daft really to come here alone
and so soon. The same scene —
trees and brambles stumbling down
to a stream; it shines
like your skin in rain.
You're here, the spaniels know it!
Drinking the wind, they forget
the fire that's grown cold,
the dusty Wellies.

They're a friendly bunch at The White Hart
but now I can't mix like before —
it sets you apart, a loss.
At home my eye is drawn
to hairline cracks in plaster,
so many trivial things
that need to be put right.
It isn't easy settling back
in a house that's been
so badly shaken.

The colour's all washed from the woods;
the sky is a harsh laundry-blue;
something caustic has bleached
its delicate chiffon clouds.
Love's elusive stuff
has been spun, wrung out
by a rough male hand.
Without you, I'm a blank —
can't even programme
the damned washing-machine.

HOME SWEET HOME

Another birthday gone with me still single!
A girl fades fast in this bed-sitter jungle
with no engagement ring! My, that is *scary*
when I so long to settle down and marry.

What's wrong with me that men don't look my way
when all I want is just an average guy?
I'm no inverted snob so won't look down
on chinless chaps who're to the Manor born.

And they won't find I am unduly harsh
on suitors with a throbbing, thrusting Porsche?
Nor will I think the worse of any man
because Dad owns a multi-million chain.

The Coughing Major might be worth pursuing;
there's talent there that just needs redeploying.
Or Harry.....if he promised no more corgis
but warmed towards some less aggressive doggies.

A shame that Beckham got snapped up by Posh;
the rain in Spain's OK when you are flush.
There needs to be an upturn in my luck
or else I'll trawl the net with Uncle Jack.

Jack has enjoyed Eurasian brides for years;
they will do anything you ask, he swears.
Somewhere there is an apeman in a tree
who'd much prefer to set up house with me!

HOUSE BEAUTIFUL

Vi swore she'd not been told of Aunty Martha's death.
How disappointing for her pals in Coney Island
who expected snaps! But what of George,
alone now and depressed?

Instead of giving in to grief, George had re-decorated,
using such skill and artistry that 'Martha's Cottage'
made *House Beautiful,* a full centre-spread.

Today at eighty-seven George still cooks, cleans,
washes up and wears a clean shirt every day;
makes fruit-cakes and pastry too.

'Heavens to Betsy! He's hibernated all these years
in Arundel! No hobbies, friends or holidays;
just him and Martha! She must see George
before she sailed. *He should get a life.*'

We took Vi to a country pub. Alas, the sandwiches
weren't half as good as those in *any*
New York deli. But we should go ahead and eat
while she had just a glass of sherry.

A few sherries later, she poured her poison in his ear.
'But George dear, don't you feel sometimes
that you've been...well, short-changed?'
He looked my cousin in the eye.

'I've always put home first. Now Martha's gone
I tend my roses and my kitchen garden. And I like
helping people. I count myself most blessed.'

Vi's IBS flared up. Perhaps it was the sherry.
We doubted she'd make Dover. But now
she's doing Lisbon, Toulon, Rome. And soon,
please God, she'll get her arse back home.

COMMUNICATING DOORS

How easily she fits into this new savannah, absorbing
the immensity of it; wearing Africa like a coat
she'll soon shrug off and leave behind. My eyes
feast on her wholeness. She stares boldly
like the elands before they break rank for our jeep.

Perhaps a holiday that's lain in wraps so long is doomed
to disappoint. Sad when so much planning, such anticipation
have gone into this trip; its purpose being to show
my daughter an old country, breathless, steaming, raw:
her birthright and her heritage.

By her side are rucksack, sun-glasses, binoculars.
Safe in her camera are crocodiles, zebra, giraffes,
elephants, baboons....for the family at home.
Perhaps tomorrow will bring rhinoceros;
that's what the kiddies want to see on film.

She's on her mobile several times a day; the parting words
'Love you' holding a clear message
for eavesdropping mums. Don't come too close,
my real life's at home. This is re-stated
by the door between our rooms: always locked.

So much stuff stands between us, piled high on her side
of the wall. Can't we talk about it? Hardly.
I embarrass her....that's something else for which
there are no words. She was still a child
when she started to pull apart.

She says I'm 'paranoid' although I'm getting better
at not noticing how often she avoids me;
her impatience at lost spectacles, my nocturnal visits
to the toilet. Banter is what she calls this bullying
scoffing voice. My grandchildren are experts.

Our last afternoon and she seems friendlier.
Of course it could just be our homeward plane
landing at Mombassa that's improved her mood.
At least she gives me a glance now and then
and she's no longer scowling.

Over dinner I try once more to nurture whatever
might remain alive between us. Is it by accident
that my tomato juice bursts into flames and burns
my throat? I promised not to get emotional
....but a child's imploring now.

Please, please look at me! Say you love me!

Six words swallow up the bongo drums,
the Leopard Beach Hotel, the whole Indian Ocean.
"Mum, do you regret adopting me?"

THE GOOD LIFE

Hauling myself from sofa, G and T and *Country Living*
I stoop to save some scrap of sodden fur
the cat just brought indoors.
Mau dares it to escape,
then bats it round the floor.

Clutched loosely in a chiffon square, such weightlessness
is touching. That feisty upturned snout,
those eyes, speak to my heart.
Claws rake down my shin:
Mau's dispossessed. And fraught.

The pipistrelle can't wait to fly. But are those wings
unpierced, airworthy still? It's hunt
or starve to death in hours.
Released it soars; its cries
soon too faint for human ears.

Back to my drink and watch the News. More refugees
with everything in one precarious pram.
Have I become too proud
of my designer clothes,
the BMW parked outside?

Perhaps tonight I will forego my bedtime stroll
in case that wrinkled sprite
lies dying in the grass.
Does such guilt have value
or one dead bat disturb the stars?

HOUSE-BOAT CHILD

HOUSE-BOAT CHILD

Edward the Transgressor	29
Love from Chloe	30
Unspeakable Cat	31
House-Boat Child	32
Survivors	34
Sleeping Leopards	35
To the Lighthouse...Again	36
...Moving House	37
Swan Island	38
Aguadulce	39
Make War, Not Love	40
Mothering Sunday	41
A Broader Church	42

EDWARD THE TRANSGRESSOR

What Edward does, he does advisedly;
like leaving white hairs
on my dark clothes,
and dark hairs on my light.

When it's raining hard
he teeters on the threshold
thrashing his long, wet tail
neither in nor out.

With an impresario's sense of timing
he will bring up fur-balls
or produce a partly-eaten mouse
just as I carve the Sunday roast.

A cat like Edward only claws
the best upholstery; satisfied
at last, he leaps up on my chest
and rubs his bum across my face.

Then he rolls on his back to present
his soft white belly-fur; all's
forgiven as I kiss his square pate
and once more clear the slate.

LOVE FROM CHLOE

What inebriate deity clothed her in gold, snow and sable
twinned gentle brown eyes with incisors bent
on destruction; then added a tail
that is death to Crown Derby! Surely
the gods must have meant
a lizard, a lion, a scorpion even;
not this clown with white ruff
and the soul of Lord Byron.
Howsoever, a corgi was born.

Half asleep by the fire, legs in air, she flutters
a limp warm paw when Lassie's on screen.
Moods look up after a romp
in fox-muck! But my smile disappears
when I find her completing
my crossword. There are
lessons to learn, rules to enforce:
corgis sometimes appear
to forget they're not people.

She is quite amazingly craven. It takes only a duck
to quack, a duster to fall, or a cat to hiss
from a wall, and she's seized
by the Rescue Dog *angst* that is marring
her safe snug life in this house.
But she's bonded like glue.
Well isn't she sitting in my armchair,
wearing my shoes, perusing
my Baudelaire...even Larousse!

Sucked socks, chewed biros, Tipp-Ex swallowed whole;
plus my man's been gone all of two days.
Chloe has bloat, she's rolling
her eyes. With him out of the way
she's back on my bed. Maybe
she is writing a poem.
To judge by her brow a Sestina
is forming. No wonder
she has a bad pain in the gut.

UNSPEAKABLE CAT

A reek of dead fish and nights on the tiles
and a purr that's a terrible sound.
You're such an unspeakable cat.

You're such an unspeakable cat. The birds
and the mice live in permanent fear
of your teeth and your claws.

Your teeth and your claws. The damage you did
to our crockery, curtains, antiques!
Those magnificent cabriole legs!

Those magnificent cabriole legs. And the wear
and the tear on our nerves was unfair.
Plus you sprayed on the floor —

yes, you sprayed on the floor though we said
don't do that. You gave us a glare
and you moved in next-door.

You moved in next-door and they worship you there!
But milk jugs and sparrows still fall —
and now we have no cat to blame.

HOUSE-BOAT CHILD

With Father gone and Mother full of gin, it wasn't easy
being a house-boat child. Cramped galley.
Makeshift wiring. Emptying bath-water
only on a falling tide. Seldom going to school.

But Battersea Reach was never dull. Ships' hooters.
A wrecked barge showing its chine. Mussels cooking
in an iron pot. No-one knew about her friend;
the one the other rats called Boss.

Why risk a clout for telling lies? She *knew*
how big he was in every way. Knew he could talk;
would sometimes sing to her —
how those high notes split her heart.

When she was ten a baulk of timber holed *Sweet Thames*,
they said the river police gave her the kiss of life;
she knew different, had felt those crossed front teeth
smelt that seductive breath.

The foul water left her with diphtheria; she might have died
in hospital on shore but for a careless snatch
of river-song, bubbling free to open her throat for life.
Sweet Thames was laid up longer than herself.

Though she saw less of Boss, she still heard his song.
Then, on her Wedding Day she quite distinctly
caught his smile reflecting off the silverware,
half-glimpsed the stacked-up presents move.

He didn't like the jellied eels, complained the porter
made him sneeze—but he was pleased
to find the newly-weds
had rented a boat on Battersea Reach.

Her three boys swam as strongly as ship's rats;
their crossed front teeth corrected by cosmetic dentistry.
When they played her up, she'd threaten to tell *him* —
that frightened more than any human father.

She's widowed now. Her sons have gone their individual ways.
The power-station's clad in primrose mist.
Across the river, Boss opens his eyes and yawns.
Yesterday he wasn't half this size!

"Come on Woman, swim across" he shouts. "You'll be with me
in a tail-shake. Then we can sing the river-song
as a duet. I'll leave you the low notes,
while I take up the high."

SURVIVORS

How fat you've grown on shoreline pickings!
Burgers, crisps, vanilla ices —
all the detritus of a seaside town.

But scavenging like this is only feather-deep!
You are the birds of ice and fire,
survivors from prehistory.

Your wildness wells and keens in me
I feel the shapely wings unfold.
Do I dream or fly

over the half-remembered shores
where aurochs grazed
and history blazed from shared fires?

You were always opportunists. Rather than drown
in diesel, you're flying back
the way you came

to where your cousins drop like stones
to snatch their dinner
from the sea,

and where the children play barefooted still
on sand so firm, so clean —
while overhead gulls dive and scream.

SLEEPING LEOPARDS

"Please Emily, say that's a leopard-skin and not the real thing!"
It's best these dimity ladies should not see me
stroke your head and call you Sister.
A well-timed visit, this! I'd come so near
to giving up. Although in certain slants of light —
despite my Mentor's poor regard —
I *knew* my verses were alive.

I get scant sympathy from you when I play Queen of Calvary.
You say there's something in me courts disaster,
else why select Charles Wadsworth
when everybody knows that he's
a married man? And why choose a Mentor
skilled in grammar, rhyme and metre
but with no eye for mystery?

One should let sleeping leopards lie. But snoozing's hard
when Mr. H throws scraps of stale scrag-end
and Preacher starts to sermonise.
One day you'll skip the mutton-scraps
and eat the hand instead; or lure the Calvinist
down paths where I mayn't tread,
except perhaps as a *voyeur*.

So now you long for home! Though nothing rivals Amherst
in the fall! You always were a creature of swift
moods! Well Ethiopia is welcome
to your sisterly advice, your gravelly purr.
But how it splits my heart to know
that soon another Sappho
will wear your spotted gown.

TO THE LIGHTHOUSE... AGAIN

Still she rises from the sea, that stark straight Venus
carrying a torch for same-sex love,
dreaming of Orlando or the Bloomsbury
Gang. The waves are sluggish now,
but my boat's heart
is more buoyant than mine.

What makes me think I've found that important other
when Vee mayn't even remember my name?
I read her like a paperback—
all that fuss about absence and loss!
Maybe too much sea
has finally drowned her brain.

Now I will rest on my oars, attend to my blisters,
bail out more water, eat my packed lunch,
hope for a breeze, imagine
the icon of motherhood five fathoms
down. And a life
without men or male values.

If I've done my sums right, I should land on the rock
just as evening falls. I must watch how I go
in that strange half-light,
lest I trample on pale silk underwear
laid on flat stones
to dry, then quite forgotten.

Gifts have to be right. I'll forget the food parcel,
give her this signed Francis Dodd instead.
Any moment now a light
will shine out. But will I discover Vee
in the tower? Or some
righteous and brass-beaked harpy?

...MOVING HOUSE

Edward Thomas moved house ten times in seventeen years, perhaps seeking to forestall bouts of recurring depression. He was killed in action at Arras in 1917, aged 39.

He moved house frequently but gloom would not be left behind.
His fast train stopped at Adlestrop just once
But then he blew his one big chance
To look around, explore. Did he half fear
That this was not a real place he saw
But more a metaphor, a cry
For all the things which passed him by
Like feeling loved and good inside, and knowing peace of mind?

I, too, soon learnt how hard it is to leave the past behind.
No cuckoo calling through the wild sweet air
Could wean me from my own despair.
I never looked for Adlestrop but came
To understand the power in a name.
Today, I think of Adlestrop
Not as a circle on a map
But rather as some special spot unique in each man's mind.

SWAN ISLAND

Shame on you Swan, for growing fat and sleazy.
It comes of gliding round an ornamental lake
and taking life too easy. You should be browsing
on lush water weeds, not guzzling stale bread.

Yet I have seen you stretch your neck and sigh,
then rise up in the water, flapping noisily;
that's when you ply your otherness, show me
you have the wildness in you still, the yearning.

But what's this shadow overhead! Am I another
Leda, to be snatched and ravished in mid-air?
But she had lover's breasts and smelt of honey,
I'm old, rheumaticky and possibly dementing.

Your massive orange bill is quietly re-arranging
my two shoulder blades. A speck of blood, no more
I swear! And I am changing to some mutant being
that's not exactly Bewick Swan.....nor woman.

Well if this is your Swan Heaven, I'm Pavlova!
No TV or radio. No Wimbledon or Service Stations.
No Jehovah's Witnesses. And where's the sharp
contentiousness that gives a Londoner more edge?

On the other hand, your cousins do look spry.
Life's more frugal in the wild. These Whooper swans
have had to fly across the North Atlantic.
And now there's not an ounce of fat between them.

Unhappily, so many things at home are shrouded still,
like terrorism, global warming. Perhaps I will stay
after all. That is, if I'm allowed. Your welcome is
assured, the likes of me must undergo a body-search.

They want no trouble on Swan Island. Security is strict.
Suppose I were an agitator! Worse, a suicide bomber!
My mind is playing tricks today. I'm all wired up
but can't seem to remember how to detonate myself!

AGUADULCE

We don't think much of the hygiene here,
the agua's far from dulce.
I wasn't aware that dead dogs smile;
yours is the same toothy grin
that you wore all through
your short unloved unlamented life.

Many dogs are washed up here. They're collected
by van, lest some untoward corpse
should prompt the hotel-guests
to seek another paradise.
For you, any attention is better
than none, even the beach man's cursing.

Thinking of you and all the drowned dogs
in this one small Spanish town,
I feel an emptiness, a shame;
shame for a lifetime of lies
and the way I died long ago
but still went on stuffing my face.

My friends are scattered or busy or disaffected.
But you would love me if you could.
So shake yourself, Friend!
Give me a chance to put food
and water down, watched
by the pale unwinking eye of the *duende*.

MAKE WAR, NOT LOVE

Of man's three brains, the oldest and most primitive is the reptile brain. It has the task of ensuring survival by alerting the body to danger.

I've always been here, curled at the base of your skull,
knowing I just had to wait. About time you woke up
to the danger, asked for my help! You're shaking
like an old woman, now the barbarians are at the gate.

Well it's good you're starting to see things my way
but remember *I* call the shots. Stag parties must end!
All that sex stuff reduces my energy. And stay away
from the Buddha. Tinfoil halos hurt my eyes.

Remember, you're either with us or for the terrorists.
No more flipping weakly between your three brains;
the other two are rubbish anyway. If it wasn't for me
you'd never have noticed the world is re-arming.

Don't think I live just in your skull. I've infiltrated
the outer world now; found weapons of mass destruction
in barns, bunkers, underground silos. I was right.
Every one of the missiles is pointing directly at us!

Not to worry Friend, I'm ex-S.A.S., one of the best.
I can see into terrorists' minds; I know which flight
has the bomb, which letters are anthrax-carriers:
don't worry, we'll counter with something stronger.

What will we do when the very last barbarian is slain
and no-one opposes our armies? Have maggots got into
your brain! Aren't there other cities, countries,
whole planets? And friends who can turn into enemies?

MOTHERING SUNDAY

No glittery cards, no calls, no *Interflora* van.
My world is shrinking fast.
I must be thankful

though for health, and for those excellent ladies
who wash me, bring me meals
and medicine, change my library books;

thankful too that I can keep my Chloe.
Some retirement homes restrict
their residents to goldfish or canaries.

Who was it said old age is not so bad?
Well I agree, it seems like that
when you consider the alternative.

But still, I would have liked a bunch of flowers
to show that someone somewhere
thinks of me on Mother's Day.

Chloe has been 'done.' Illogical to mourn
those panting back door suitors,
the unborn pups.

Still wobbly from the anaesthetic and wearing
an outrageous stiff white cone,
Chloe wags her tail

as sunlight changes plastic into sparkling cellophane:
her face peeps out like flowers —
an inspirational bouquet.

A BROADER CHURCH

A company of wolves is gathered here.
They whimper; soft noses
nuzzling my skin.

The sky is heavy with birds.
I never heard
so desperate a chorus.

A maggot crawls uncertainly
round the periphery
of my shroud.

Spades tamp home the churches' final
answer. I knelt at no
known altar,

nor loved my fellow men; preferring fur
and feather, fishes,
even horny toad or spider.

A vagrant's grave is fitting. I'm glad
there'll be no sherry,
no forgiveness,

glad too I stayed away from Mass
and hardly ever used
my given skin.

I ran with wolves, wore fur and found
no meanness there.
So if I hear the howling

of those who crossed the river first,
why then, I'll strike out
with good heart.

In wolves I've touched my own dark core:
my otherness. Through them,
a broader church.

SECRETS IN THE ATTIC

SECRETS IN THE ATTIC

Secrets in the Attic	45
The Wendy House	46
Black Dog	47
Goat-Speak	48
De Profundis	49
Evil Eye	50
Unfair	51
Inés	52
Marlene	54
No. 6 Laurel Street	55
Partridge Breasts	56
Boule de Suif	57
Shoes	58

SECRETS IN THE ATTIC

Something smells awful up here, sweet and rotten,
there's nothing that isn't tired and broken;
Action Man, stringless guitar, Lego pieces.
Wait! The Dinky toys should go to auction.

Cover all mirrors! Don't want to see my son
with tomorrow's pain written large. Bad
mistake, disturbing the dust. Should have
stayed downstairs with a night's television.

I know you're here, hiding under a mattress,
or secreting yourself in the Wendy House.
No wonder you're sweating. Don't you fancy
cobwebs for hair, pale maggots for eyes?

You know what's coming; it's settlement time,
you haven't a hope in hell, not with me cast
as Grendel's Mother. Even a flat-iron's to hand —
just the job to straighten out sluts like you.

Am I doing this bad thing for me or my son?
I've hated you in his loving embrace —
what would the neighbours say if they knew
this was one of those mother-son things?

But why in hell am I justifying myself to you?
He was always a good son till you came along.
This is the proof that you have bewitched him:
it's a week, and he hasn't come near me.

THE WENDY HOUSE

Your third child accidentally dead! Might that
be overdoing it a bit? Well I shan't say a word.
I know those terrible twos can suck you dry;
it gets worse with the threes and fours. Girls?

Richmal Crompton said it all with one called
Violet Elizabeth Bott. But boys are just as beastly.
A second child to keep the first one company?
You're joking! Anthea was sick-making enough.

Good planning scored. We showed up faithfully
at nursery school, bought Early Learning toys,
sat through McDonald's awful birthday parties,
then came out squeaky clean on parent-ratings!

And luck was kind! Our old discarded freezer
waiting for collection; her Wendy House, she said.
We shed buckets, wrote the manufacturer, went
on television...did the grieving parents thing.

Forget that rot about a guilty heart. Look at us!
We party when we please and lie in bed all hours.
No more obnoxious twos, threes, fours or fives.
We put fresh flowers on little Anthea's grave.

BLACK DOG

Orange combat pants and purple lips.
Blanche laughed like a hyena.
The whole world knew about her rather
special gift for friendship. 'Darling this'
and 'Darling that.' Her tongue

was in so many cheeks. With same-sex things
there's an intensity. Blanche couldn't
wait to turn my life around.
She *knew* about depression. Just say
'Black Dog' and she would come to me!

Was this the dog that rode around
on Oscar's shoulders? The dog that smelt
of moonbeams and wet leaves? That comforted
Virginia Woolf and Plath as they stood
listening to sad music?

Blanche tried to heal so many friends;
she spun round like a Catherine wheel.
'Black Dog's on top of me' I wailed.
But in every pack there's at least one rocket
that splutters a bit, then fizzles out.

What's the point of always running, running
from my own four-footed shadow?
Without the wholeness Black Dog brings
I think my loneliness might worsen.
Tonight we'll bury Blanche:

her grave shall say she was a learning curve.
Black Dog will sing the hymns,
his voice is earthy, *basso profundo*.
I begged her to sing for me; but she
was a Roman Candle burning for someone else.

GOAT-SPEAK

Is it you again, Friend, yellow eyes glaring;
hair full of straw; reeking as though
you sleep in that coat;
lager cans bulging your pockets?

How did you slip through the dream-net
while the rest of us sat at our looms
spinning the stuff of poetry,
carefully watching the Muse's lips?

We glimpsed you out there in the grounds,
suffering, proud, not sharing
our space or our food,
not helping us sing the creation.

The instructions she'd given were clear:
'Write. No lifting your pens
until I say stop!' Only
a ploy to help the words flow.

But you had to annoy her, ask 'why?'
We next saw you sniffing a rose,
saying this was the only poem
you felt like writing that day.

Talking to flowers was OK. Stuffing them
into your mouth was *gross*.
Somebody said it only took one
to spoil a whole course.

When we saw those two lumps on your forehead
and you started to walk on all fours,
that's when we wrote the letter
saying we wanted you gone.

Eyes defeated, you stand at the door and knock.
Was it parched and prickly out there?
Is the week best forgotten...
or should we move on to goat-speak?

DE PROFUNDIS

It's good you let your students call you simply Jock.
Your Serbo-Croat name is unpronounceable. But so
romantic. You've been a language teacher; barman:
dustman and potato picker somewhere near Slavonsky
Brod. Also poet-in-residence at two English prisons
and a training school for clergy. Now you lecture
at a Scottish University and Chair *The Burns Society,*
plus you teach this Adult Education evening class.

Less is more, you say. But still we lard our work
with vagueness, generality, abstractions. You speak
of metaphor; Ross thinks it is some kind of butterfly.
You might have guessed the word *anthropomorphic*
would be beyond Fiona. Kirstie blushed tomato red
when told that her first menstrual blood was private,
personal and boring. It was no subject for a poem,
you said. Wrong. Vicki Feaver got away with it.

Your new collection DE PROFUNDIS is far too deep
for me. So many scholarly allusions. Line-breaks
which bring my asthma on. Still, I paid my £7.99
so mean to persevere. By the way, I like the slant
of your felt hat. *That* speaks of raw immediacy
and poetry with a fierce fresh eye. You've won some
meaningful awards. Not the Forward Prize as yet;
but never mind, you're sure to get it next time round.

They say you're humping Mona Scaddle, the girl from
Inverurie with carrot hair and freckles. She doesn't
have a brain in her whole body. Tutors shouldn't mess
with students. But we're in a disempowered situation
and can only mutter maledictions. *May your trews
contain just balls of screwed-up poems. May your affair
with Il Postino come to nothing.* O wad some Pow'r
the giftie gie us to all have breasts like Mona Scaddle.

EVIL EYE

Nescio quis teneros oculus mihi fascinat agnos. Virgil.

I watch and wait. The lambs round here
seem plagued by some unearthly fear
as if they'd seen the Evil Eye;
the cosset lambs are first to die.
And something's ailing my career,

I miss promotion every year.
There's such a spiteful atmosphere!
I hardly dare to question why.
I watch and wait.

My wife and child will not come near.
There's not a soul who holds me dear;
and little lambs, once blithe and spry,
start having fits when I pass by.
The grieving ewes blame me, that's clear.
I watch and wait.

UNFAIR

I do hope my Sonny won't choose the wrong crowd
        or join in some brawl
                or fall foul of the Law.
He's promised to buy me
        a headsquare to hide
                the ageing effects of white hair.

Dear, O dear, he's met some old pals at the fair.
        That's Sandra I'm sure
                on the blue rocking-horse
with her lips far too close
        to his gold-pendant ear:
                her suggestions are bound to be coarse.

We've had miserable luck ever since moving here.
        It began when he decked
                that Norwegian Au Pair.
She called him a loser —
        well, she was a mare
                and of course she had flaming red hair.

Dear, O dear, that Sandra's a right nosy bitch!
        She'll keep on at him now
                till he shows her the spot
where he did for the lass
        who protested too much —
I'm afraid she'll be starting to rot.

Uprooting ourselves is the worst kind of bore.
        But we're packing again
                for a new midnight flight.
Sonny's so headstrong:
        I ask is it <u>fair</u>
                that at forty my hair has gone white?

INÉS

After Baltasar Del Alcázar

For one whole year my heart was held in thrall
by a most delightful whore called Inés.
And if by chance she had a richer client,
why then that night I laid her in my dreams.
I had eyes for her alone. She taught me
all a young man needs to know of love;
I felt no wish for further solace.

One day the dear girl set an unexpected meal
before me. (Whores often have this warm
and generous streak). All her ingredients
were the finest; nor had she stinted labour.
She'd cooked a succulent side of ham,
then served it with dark purple aubergines;
the whole dish swam in melted cheese.

This was *haute cuisine!* My senses swooned
at the aroma. Inés was of course the first
to have her joy of me; that is her triumph,
hers alone. But nothing stays the same for ever.
Unhappily, my soul's now torn apart
by not one love but three; each one of whom
demands to be preferred above the others.

Unfair to ask me which of my three charmers
I love best — Inés, the kind-hearted whore;
those juicy slices of roast ham; or aubergines
in cheese. Inés has breasts that make men
faint. The ham comes all the way from Aracena;
the cheese is Andalusia's best; I'm dribbling
now, just thinking of those aubergines.

Trying to judge between these three has basted
me with sweat. And still their finer points
are so precisely balanced in my mind, with due
regard to warmth, smell, nourishment and flavour,
that I'm no longer certain which is Inés,
which smoked ham, which *berengenas con queso*.
I drown in smoky sensuous cheese sauce.

I'm glad this contest has no outright winner,
no gallant losers nursing their bruised egos.
All the same, the healthy bite of competition
should work to my advantage. Once Inés knows
that Aracena ham, and aubergines in cheese,
are rivalling her in my affections, she's sure
to offer me her favours at a lower tariff.

MARLENE

Her phone box ad says twenty-five. (She's nearer
thirty-seven). The punters come all ages;
Victor's purple Y-fronts don't do him any
favours; his underarms are seriously sweaty.

What a rush the fellow's in! No time for pleasantries
like foreplay. He doesn't even ask her name.
It's obvious he's gone without for quite some time —
such waiting's worth at least another twenty!

"Look out," she warns, more tickled than alarmed,
"You're far too near the edge. Any minute now
you'll topple off and break your bloody arm."
"Don't care if I do!" His little-boy bravado

reminds her of her son, fostered out since birth.
Now Victor gets a genuinely loving love-bite;
she's forgotten in this broody moment how easily
such white unwholesome skin can bruise.

"Stop that, you daft cow. Do you want my fiancée
to find your marks on me? Where's the sodding
shower?" "Over there. And please don't leave
the place awash. My next is here in half an hour."

"All paid for then?" he asks emerging, farting.
"You still owe me twenty. Now don't make trouble,
Darling. You know my rates." "But you said fifty
on the phone." Her lips smile, her eyes do not.

"I'm sorry, Luv. You must've heard me wrong.
Fifty's my charge for massage and then oral sex;
you had intercourse as well, remember Luvvy?"
"I've no more cash! Plastic? Sorry, left at home."

Gone! Leaving behind his Marks and Spencer snack
plus a pair of Ratner earrings gift-wrapped
for his intended. The earrings she drops in the bin
...then sets to work on the prawn sandwich.

No. 6 LAUREL STREET

Tourists ask for Homer. He's part of Blandford Forum
like the Corn Exchange. He wears a black Fedora;
haunts Nelson's Wine Bar, Scruples.
Some folk laugh behind their hands at what
they please to call his tired themes,
bathetic phrases, clunking
rhymes. They call him McGonagall 2.

How crass to belittle *Railway Bridge of the Silv'ry Tay!*
Disaster's a serious business. Homer knows;
he underwrites suspension bridges.
Well Blandford Forum should remember
that beneath a Lloyds persona
may throb a poet's soul.
What better address than Laurel Street!

Homer doesn't care for gloom. He's up for Betjeman
and positive women like *Joan Hunter Dunn.*
But sometimes JB lets him down;
take that couple in the Bath tea-shop,
their love is plainly doomed!
Homer dislikes that poem;
he wants just the icing, a love-affair

that lasts forever. Tourists tend to tread more carefully
as they draw near the square where poems
are famously graven on stone.
Homer's feet haven't learnt to read!
Words can be slippery —
he's warned. Yet every time
he trips exactly on that paving stone.

PARTRIDGE BREASTS

***anecdote attributed to Horace Walpole,
Brewer's Dictionary of Phrase and Fable***

A certain King in ancient France
was prone to play unpleasant tricks
on that good priest who chided him
for so much out-of-wedlock sex.

"What food do you like best, my friend?"
the Monarch one day asked the priest
who guilelessly replied that he
was partial to a partridge breast.

The crafty King gave orders then
that his old friend should only eat
the thing he'd said he most preferred,
served always on a golden plate.

For luncheon, supper, breakfast, tea
they stuffed the partridge down him till
he came to hate his favourite dish;
it made him heave, it made him quail.

Long weeks elapsed before the King
relented slightly and enquired
if everything was to his taste
and if he thought he'd been well served.

Still green from partridge poisoning,
the poor old man just found the words
to say that now he'd had his fill
of that most succulent royal bird.

The King said "Ah, you take my point;
the stomach craves variety
and it is just the same with sex.
So stuff all that morality!

"My queen has breasts to make men swoon
but she alone can't satisfy
a high sex drive like mine. God save
us from *perdrix, toujours perdrix*"

BOULE DE SUIF

He envied Flaubert, Daudet, Zola
for churning out such powerful stuff.
Poor Maupassant felt dwarfed by them,
<u>his</u> work was not profound enough.

The world was failing him as well;
such meanness and such prudery!
He found it the working class
...he found in the *bourgeoisie!*

His first nouvelle was far the best.
Thank God he died not knowing that
his fame would largely rest upon
a Paris whore called Mutton Fat.

SHOES

We had not wished him dead, that poor
deluded Nazarene,
and to this day I seem to hear
a hammer in my brain.

We liked what we had seen of him
although we'd always known
that in the end he'd self-destruct;
he just could not dumb down.

At first like all the other lads
he learnt his father's trade,
grew skilful with the adze and plane —
but Oh, that swollen head.

His mother's eyes were dark with fear.
She scolded when she heard
him boasting to the other kids
he was the son of God.

A few years on...and he would beg
his so-Old Testament dad
to pardon us for killing him —
not knowing what we did.

Not knowing what we did! He shamed
us with that worn excuse;
we felt like something less than men,
hearing him plead for us.

Blocking our ears as best we could,
we fell to casting lots,
for that's the Roman soldier's way
of settling who gets what.

My luck was in. Or did I cheat?
Mine was the greatest prize,
but then I slunk away barefoot.
How could I wear his shoes?

HOUSE OF THE LEFT-HAND DOOR

HOUSE OF THE LEFT-HAND DOOR

House-To-House Salesman	61
Carousel Man	62
Asylums	64
Waiting For The Inspectors	65
Judy's House	66
A Squidgy Fellow	67
Sea Change	68
The Moldavian Army Women's Choir	69
Ghost Town	70
Reflections	71
House of the Left-Hand Door	72

HOUSE-TO-HOUSE SALESMAN

Listen to the starlings arguing. All that counts
is pecking order in this leafy lane
with wrought iron entry gates.

Notice how the houses are all architect-designed.
They're loaded here and spoilt for space;
even their lawns are manicured.

Imagine all the labour that has shaped this topiary
plus the cost of Grecian Goddesses
in white Italian marble.

Look Matey, I'm not trying to give you grief.
All I'm saying is doorstep salesmen
won't get a foot in here.

Your smile says you've had it tough. You've sold
protection to the Bombay beggars:
five annas to sleep safe.

Life's pleasant and predictable in Woodcote Avenue.
Koi carp grow fat in ornamental pools,
the kids all have a pony.

Fine Wilton flows through all the houses here,
soft lakes in which a cat might drown.
Who needs Kashmiri rugs?

Your smile remains undented. It says that you
could sell a tiger skin
to Wild Life conservationists.

Hang about. Why don't the two of us swap loads?
Then you could shift a few of these
Encyclopedia Britannicas.

CAROUSEL MAN

He helped her mount the lion with shaggy mane,
then rode the unicorn beside her. Mum felt
a deep distrust of fair-ground folk
especially didicois like Brishan.

She pointed to the peeling paint, snarling curs,
the litter. That carousel looked quite
unsafe! Fairs were dangerous places.
The child saw just the candyfloss, the glitter.

Miss Plum watched her smile as she slid
down the rope, eyes closed. Ah, these wicked
new sensations! The verbal flogging
from her P.E. teacher.

But after school Brishan's arms were kind.
"Cheer up, Sweetpea. Don't mind the likes of her.
One day I'll kiss you there; then you'll know
what that old sow was on about."

After that, he kept a lower profile…but he was there
when Mother died. Lately Mum had seemed
to fill the house; he snapped his fingers twice
and *punkt* she came back down to size.

Almost grown-up now, she made a play for Brishan.
It was too soon. Fair-ground life could be
tough, he warned, especially for women.
"Tough in what way?" she wanted to know.

Fair-men worked a woman hard but didn't show her
much regard. Complete subservience was demanded:
there wasn't a man who would start the day's work
till his woman knelt to tie his laces.

Was he ribbing? You could never tell with Brishan.
Well it was time she learnt to do without him.
All in six months, she married Arthur, enrolled
at Uni, took up prison-visiting and fell for Frank.

Her new husband quailed. All this studying,
scraped toast, housework on permanent hold,
a temper matching her flame tresses. Now ex-cons
coming to tea. Arthur wanted a divorce.

Pregnant next. And not even Arthur's child!
She'd have liked a baby, but how unfair on this
particular kid! A recidivist for Dad. Herself
at risk for HIV; Frank's legacy of course.

Brishan's kiss was fierce and hard. "Poor
old Moo!" was all he said. His treasured watch
immediately joined their funds....now she
could look for a back-street abortion.

*

Botched. Someone sponged her hot dry skin,
brushed her eyelids with his lips.
She thought she heard the carousel organ,
smelt engine-oil. Then she saw Brishan cry.

*

One pall-bearer is taller than the others,
which lends wry humour to this grave procession.
There's difficulty lowering the coffin.
Someone laughs. Two people walk away.

The carousel will turn again, the night sky
burn with neon stars. Is this the ride
that lasts for ever; with him astride the unicorn
and her beside him on the lion?

ASYLUMS

They aren't called that now. But that's where
my sister-by-marriage spent most of her life;
in one of those Victorian mausoleums set far back
from the world. She was less than twenty-one
the day they took her away.

She embarrassed her family, but she had beauty
talent, wit. She wanted to be a concert pianist;
might have succeeded too, except for odd quirks
like boxing her music teacher's ears. This was
turn of the century Edinburgh,

and mental illness spoilt her sisters' marriage chances.
Committed as soon as her father died (she'd been
his darling) Hetty ceased to exist. But compassion
was shown in the asylum they chose; it possessed
a grand piano where she could practise.

It was hard, marrying into this stern Scottish family
where a sister's name must never be spoken.
But she wasn't going anywhere. And not many
asylums boasted a Steinway. I got there
in time for her seventieth birthday.

They'd dressed her neatly, brushed her hair.
Tactless to ask about her music. Blank faces
left me wondering if the piano had ever existed.
But Hetty would know, surely she would
remember practising on it?

She dodged my questions and my embraces.
Rebuffed, I asked Matron if Hetty might have
the scones I'd brought. "Oh yes," she said
"She'll like that. Hetty's partial to scones."
She ate them all. Paper bag as well.

WAITING FOR THE INSPECTORS

With apologies to Cavafy

Why are we waiting hour after hour in Assembly?
And why have the usual staff meetings been cancelled?

> Because the inspectors arrive today. It's better
> *they* draw up the guidelines, set the new targets.

Why did the Head get up early to have her hair done
and why is she wearing her cap and gown?

> Because the inspectors arrive today and she will
> present their top man with a scroll
> showing how we've improved in the tables.

Why is Miss Jones wearing Next and Mr. Lamont his Public
School tie? Why have they polished the cups and blown up
balloons and laid red Axminster down?

> Because the inspectors arrive today and they always
> enjoy a bit of bamboozle.

But why all the pushing and shoving? Why is the building
emptying so fast?

> Because it's gone four and we've not been inspected.
> And we've heard from reliable Government sources
> that inspectors are being phased out.

We thought of them once as invaders but how swiftly
they slipped into parent role! Remove the red carpet.
Sound funeral drums. For nothing now can ever be the same.

JUDY'S HOUSE

That's my son, coming in a hired van to fetch me.
Bring my bits and bobs, he said, but not too many.
Got to downsize now. Judy, where's my sodding
keys? Silly me! Shan't need this bunch again,

and Judy's gone...gone for good this time.
Trouble is, I miss the miserable old punch-ball;
but then again, she never knew a woman's place.
I should have decked her harder, oftener!

Sonny says it's not too late to change my mind.
I can still say no to *Evergreen Retirement Homes.*
But do I have a choice? This will always feel
like Judy's house. What do you say to a ghost?

Perhaps if I went somewhere new I might feel less
like half a Punch and Judy show. Nothing's
left in this old house to get me going now. No
fights about the telly. No-one to blame or chivvy.

She had her uses, that one. Chopping wood, bringing
in the coal, lifting me in and out of the bath.
Strong, my Judy was. Once she broke my arm.
And I'm supposed to be the violent one!

I'd be the death of her, she swore. Well she
was wrong. She left this house bruised and minus
a few teeth...but with plenty of fight in her still.
The dog fared worse. So far I've spared her bird.

All day long it shrieks: 'Who's a silly boy then?'
Must wring its useless neck. It can't do any
of the things that Judy did, like find my socks
and put them on my feet while I still lie in bed.

A SQUIDGY FELLOW

A white-washed outhouse stored the season's glut;
you reached the upper floor by ladder —
it was cool and dark.

Twelve-dozen trays would tremble as Pa climbed
the rungs. My, was he a stickler!
He hit my head

with the first one he rejected; a squidgy fellow,
anxious brown and mildewy,
too soft for life.

Ma hovered anxiously below:
her part and mine came later —
peeling, coring, slicing.

She'd pack the half-moons into Kilner jars,
boiling them in a copper pan,
then sealing their necks with wax.

Was it really so idyllic? Why can't I still enjoy
juice dribbling down my chin?
The average man

remembers boyhood as a thousand sweet crisp apples.
My thoughts alight like wasps
on the few no-hopers.

Years ago I asked Pa if it was just luck
which apples turned out well
and which were rotten at the core?

He's gone. So I can't ask him why my brain
is now a thoroughfare
for colonies of pale fat maggots.

SEA CHANGE

after Antonio Machado

A clock strikes. A spade drives deep and clean.

Here is a space where a man might lie
alone with himself
and the sound of the sea.

Best get myself home before that long trench
takes a liking to me.

My fingers grow chill. My toes are numb.
I'm losing my centre, losing my hold
on the books and the cushions
the firelight, the smells
which tell me I've been here,
I've lived in this house by the sea.

But Death comes tender. He promises me
no water shall touch my hair or my brow
and I shall not know or remember
crossing the sea.

I will sleep a long time on the other shore.
Then my eyes will be open
      and open
and I'll see that my boat
is made fast nearby
in the place where I am
      and I am.

The things which I held so dear will be picked
by the gulls and washed by the waves
and cast up changed
     on the sand.

THE MOLDAVIAN ARMY WOMEN'S CHOIR

Now they're assembling on the stage;
no virgin choir this,
but weathered partisans.
I like to see their sallow noses
glow with perspiration.
I like to hear them raise
those grainy Slavic voices
in praise of love and poetry
and war with rascally neighbours.

There's buggers in white coats who want
to take my cataracts away.
My eyesight suits me fine.
I can see what their eyes can't:
I can see through khaki.
I can see these ladies
are just waiting to get laid.
Why else would they be mother naked
and giving me the glad eye?

GHOST TOWN

Ol' man river knows how it feels, being tired of living
and scared of dying. Scared to death of what waits
on the other side, afraid of the harpies, the scolds
who're longing to sink their teeth in her flesh
and settle old scores. She's ready to answer for all
the mean things she did; small infelicities and betrayals.
Oh but she dreads the lies that flap round like pigs
in a wallowing sky. Such a nasty game, Chinese Whispers.

There are men who'll allege she pricked their balloons,
that she never sent any chap home to his wife
feeling bigger and better than Schwarzenegger.
There are grown-up kids, still oozing original slime,
who'll swear their noses hardly ever got wiped
since she tended her animals first. There are women
who'll claim she spoilt every hen-thing she went to —
they called her a sex-change waiting to happen.

Angry young men have charm. Stroppy old women
have none, too many white hairs on the chin.
Maybe what's needed is just a fresh start. Perhaps
she'll grow roots in Ghost Town, dumb down, learn
to fit in, take advice, give confrontation a rest.
Well now, here's a to-do! Something is stirring
below. Maybe it's time for a Coming Out party;
but should she dress on the left or the right?

REFLECTIONS

The stranger who's been idling all afternoon
beside the waterlily pool
works chewed lips as if to ask
some crucial question
of the child.

A sudden frisson in the air makes him huddle
deeper into his anonymous
greatcoat. That soft brown hair,
those pallid wispy arms,
are hazily familiar.

If only she would speak! It takes some time
to clear his mind. Children
are seducers... but it's decent men,
clean-living men like him,
that fear prosecution.

HOUSE OF THE LEFT-HAND DOOR

This was supposed to be a fresh start. For us as well as them.
New environment. Safe. Warm. Warden-assisted.
But alas, no Chinese take-away! You'd never think Mum drove
an ambulance...or that Dad was a Changai Jail survivor.

They want to live with us! Imagine the smell, the infirmities
of old age. And not feeling free to watch our adult movies.
All that they talk about now is China, a land where parents
can count on soft rice and a permanent chair by the fire.

Once perhaps, but now there's a population out of control,
a geriatric survivors' problem. But China builds higher!
Highest of all is House of the Left-Hand Door, reserved
for honourable pensioners. It vanishes into the sun's red eye.

Container gardening is encouraged. But only ice-white flowers
are allowed: Madonna lilies, snow-on-the mountain, ox-eye
daisies. Best tread carefully on the balconies. One or two cases
of weak balustrades, cement with a touch too much sand.

The décor's all white on the highest level. Altzheimer's white.
At first we worried that white was the colour of mourning,
but our son, who's a trainee mortician, says white also stands
for resurrection...it opens doors for the living as well.